£6.95

The Hoffnung
MUSIC FESTIVAL

Books by
GERARD HOFFNUNG

Hoffnung's The Maestro
The Hoffnung Symphony Orchestra
The Hoffnung Music Festival
The Hoffnung Companion to Music
Hoffnung's Musical Chairs
Hoffnung's Acoustics

The

Hoffnung

Music Festival

Per Tuba
ad Astra.

GERARD HOFFNUNG

LONDON 2000

First published 1956
jointly by Dennis Dobson Ltd
and Putnam & Co Ltd
2nd impression February 1957
3rd impression November 1957
4th impression September 1958
5th impression September 1960
6th impression October 1962
7th impression September 1965
8th impression December 1968
9th impression December 1972
10th impression October 1975
11th impression December 1977 (Paperback)
12th impression 1978 (Paperback)
and subsequently re-published by
Souvenir Press from 1983

This edition published 2000
by The Hoffnung Partnership
44 Pilgrims Lane
London NW3 1SN
and reprinted 2004

Copyright © The Hoffnung Partnership 2000

ISBN 1 903643 02 3

Cover and book design
Vera Brice and Leslie Robinson

Printed and bound in Great Britain
by St Edmundsbury Press Ltd
Blenheim Industrial Park, Newmarket Road
Bury St Edmunds, Suffolk IP33 3TZ

To
The Morley College Symphony Orchestra
and its inspired conductor Lawrence Leonard,
with much affection.

·····———◆▬———······

Acknowledgements

Grateful thanks are due to Ronald Searle for his contribution
to this book, and also to its designers and printers for the
infinite care and consideration they have taken in its production.

Foreword

Gerard Hoffnung was indisputably a one-man band. A one-man festival of music, conducted with a cheeky flourish and a sharp little pen. It is no surprise that the musical instruments in his drawings are as much living creatures as their human scrapers, blowers and fingerers. Nor is it difficult to believe that he persuaded Dennis Brain, genius horn player, to perform a composition by Leopold Mozart on a garden hose to a full house in London's Festival Hall. In that same concert Hoffnung played second tuba, an instrument that remarkably resembled him. His physique could have been drawn by himself to mingle with some of the rotund, prematurely balding inhabitants of his drawings. Those drawings retained to the end, echoes of his childhood reading in Berlin where he was born in 1925. He was to remain a precocious, brilliant child in a life that was to end all too abruptly in London in 1959. I knew him well and was very fond of him. I still miss his laugh. Happily he still lives on in these drawings.

Ronald Searle

The Conductors

Alerto

Preciso

Con adornamento

Grandioso

Agilmente

Con fuoco

Piano

Senza batone

Slargando

Maestoso

Non troppo

Elegantemente

Sehr markiert

Sotto

Bel Canto

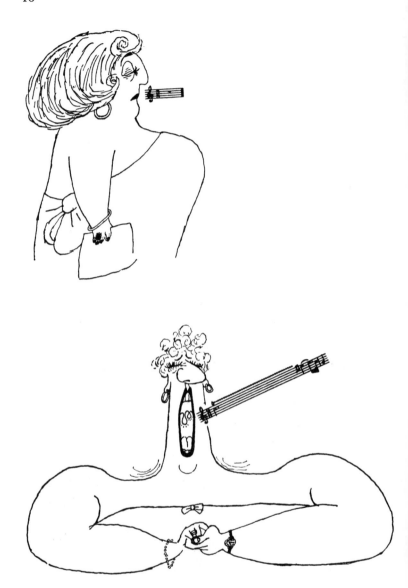

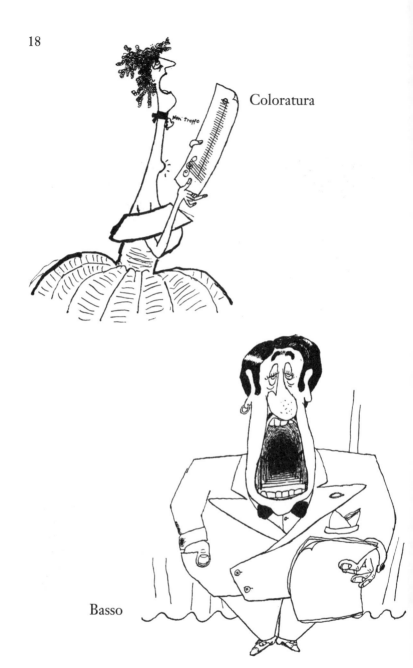

Coloratura

Basso

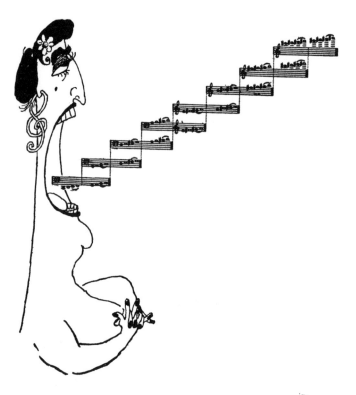

Signorina . . .
acknowledges
applause

A Sextet

The Festival Chorus

The Soloists

TV brings
the Festival
to a wider
audience

An unfortunate incident

Mainly Instrumental

The
Trout Quintet

VACUUM QUARTET IN A FLAT
(THE HOOVER)

for
two Vacuums in f
one vacuum in E Flat*
one contra vacuum in BB flat
(World première)

*If desired this may be replaced by an
electric Floor-polisher in A flat.

Con Sord*

*with mute

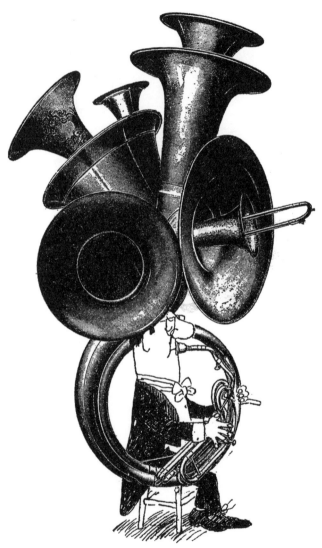

The Great Octuple Bombardon
(Americano Expresso)

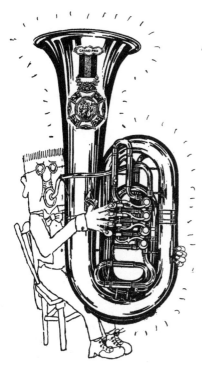

Tuba alla Tedesca

Tuba Anglais (Leeds)

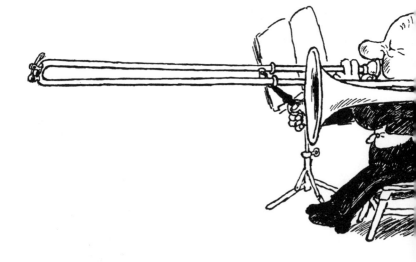

A bbb flat sub-contra-bass-
trombone-player and friend

350 Bars Rest

THE END